D1243833

Communities

Living in a
Small Town

by Lisa Trumbauer

Consulting Editor: Gail Saunders-Smith, PhD

Capstone
press

Mankato, Minnesota

Pebble Books are published by Capstone Press,
151 Good Counsel Drive, P.O. Box 669, Mankato, Minnesota 56002.
www.capstonepress.com

1 2 3 4 5 6 10 09 08 07 06 05

Library of Congress Cataloging-in-Publication Data
Trumbauer, Lisa, 1963–
    Living in a small town / by Lisa Trumbauer.
    p. cm.—(Communities)
    Includes bibliographical references and index.
    ISBN 0-7368-3633-0 (hardcover)
    1. Cities and towns—United States—Juvenile literature. I. Title.
II. Communities (Mankato, Minn.)
HT123.T78 2005
307.76'0973—dc22   2004011163

Summary: Simple text and photographs describe life in small towns.

Note to Parents and Teachers

The Communities set supports social studies standards related to
people, places, and geography. This book describes and illustrates
small towns. The images support early readers in understanding
the text. The repetition of words and phrases helps early readers
learn new words. This book also introduces early readers to
subject-specific vocabulary words, which are defined in the
Glossary section. Early readers may need assistance to read some
words and to use the Table of Contents, Glossary, Read More,
Internet Sites, and Index sections of the book.

Table of Contents

Small Towns

A small town
is a community.
A small town
is smaller than a city.

A small town
has quiet neighborhoods.
People in small towns
know many of
their neighbors.

Many small towns
have a post office
and a town hall.

Work and School

A small town
has a main street.
Some people work and
shop on the main street.

frankfort Tackle Box
FRANKFORT TACKLE BOX
WOLVERINE TACKLE
minnows
PROPELLER REPAIR

Some people work
in stores and shops
around town.
Other people drive to
a nearby city to work.

Many small towns have a library and a school.

Fun in a Small Town

Some small towns have movie theaters.
Some small towns have bowling alleys.

Small towns have parks.
Children play at the parks.

Every state has
many small towns.
Do you live
in a small town?

Glossary

community—a group of people who live in the same area

main street—a road that runs through the center of a town

neighborhood—a small area within a community where people live

post office—a place where mail is sorted and delivered

town hall—a place where the government of a town is conducted

Read More

Holland, Gini. *I Live in a Town.* Where I Live. Milwaukee: Weekly Reader Early Learning Library, 2004.

Kehoe, Stasia Ward. *I Live in a Town.* Kids in Their Communities. New York: PowerKids Press, 2000.

Nelson, Robin. *Where Is My Town?* First Step Nonfiction. Minneapolis: Lerner, 2002.

Internet Sites

FactHound offers a safe, fun way to find Internet sites related to this book. All of the sites on FactHound have been researched by our staff.

Here's how:

1. Visit *www.facthound.com*

2. Type in this special code **0736836330** for age-appropriate sites. Or enter a search word related to this book for a more general search.

3. Click on the **Fetch It** button.

FactHound will fetch the best sites for you!

Index

Word Count: 117
Grade: 1
Early-Intervention Level: 13

Editorial Credits
Mari C. Schuh, editor; Kate Opseth, designer; Jo Miller, photo researcher; Scott Thoms, photo editor

Photo Credits
Banana Stock Ltd., cover (boy in foreground); Brand X Pictures, cover (background); Bruce Coleman Inc./Carolyn Schaefer, 12; Capstone Press/Karon Dubke, 14, 20; Comstock, cover (children); Corbis/Corbis/Lee Snider, 8; Michael S. Lewis, 4; Houserstock/Dave G. Houser, 6; Houserstock/Steve Bly, 10; OneBlueShoe, 1, 16, 18